1420 mt Rose St.
Reno

St. ...
Re ...

1-19-65
Pat - John
Erwin

# THE WAY OF DISCIPLESHIP

# THE WAY

# OF DISCIPLESHIP

*The Meaning of Membership in
The United Presbyterian Church*

PUBLISHED BY
THE BOARD OF CHRISTIAN EDUCATION
OF THE UNITED PRESBYTERIAN CHURCH
IN THE U.S.A.

# Contents

# Foreword

This book is written to help persons understand what the Presbyterian Church teaches about Christian beliefs and how this church functions as one part of the universal church of Jesus Christ. The book is divided into two sections, one on beliefs, and the other on the background and practices of Presbyterianism in America today.

This book is part of the *Christian Faith and Life* curriculum for adults. Although the book will be read by individuals, it will be used most effectively as a basis for group study. It is a brief book, and the subjects it covers are developed in the ongoing adult curriculum year after year.

The way of church membership is the way of discipleship—discipleship to Jesus Christ. He is at the center of the church's beliefs, and he is Lord of the church's life. The most important result of study of this book should be a deeper personal loyalty to God's Son, whom God sent into his world to reconcile men unto himself.

# PART I

*Christian Belief*

# CHAPTER I

# The Great Invitation

Joining the church is a person's answer to an invitation. However, the invitation is not issued by the church in its own name, or by a minister or another member in his name. It is an invitation that comes from Jesus Christ. You must hear it as *his* summons to you before your membership can be meaningful.

We are separated in time by some two thousand years from the first occasions when Jesus extended his invitation to men to become his disciples. But the separation is insignificant, because the claim is still the same as it was then. A man's response to it is still decisive for his whole life. To reject it, or to be indifferent toward it, is still to deny the authority of God over a man's life and to refuse a treasure of great price. Jesus presents himself to men today, inviting them to receive him and follow him. What the church offers is not allegiance to the memory of a dead hero but discipleship to a living Lord.

We must, therefore, look at how Jesus issued the great invitation to discipleship in the days when he was on earth and hear it as *today's* invitation.

## STRANGE DISCIPLES

The men and women who became Jesus' disciples in those days were, by and large, a strange collection of people. From the point of view of good public relations for his cause, Jesus made every conceivable mistake. Instead of working hand in hand with the leaders of the people, the scribes and Pharisees, he went to men whom the Jews considered traitors: the publicans who collected taxes for the hated Romans. On the other hand, instead of aligning himself with those revolutionaries who were plotting the overthrow of Rome, he called as disciples men who had learned patience and steadfastness at their fishing trade. He could be labeled neither conservative nor radical. Yet instead of being seen in the right places, with the right people, he acquired a reputation for being particularly popular with adulterers and other sinners.

This was not because he deliberately went out of his way to shock society. He was not a social rebel who enjoyed making a spectacle of himself. In fact, it was not so much that he rejected the respectable and conventional as that respectable and conventional people rejected him and his message. His words could not pierce the thick armor that such people had built around their souls. He could be received only by those who were themselves hurt and wounded, needing a physician. People who did not know they were sick would hardly call him in. He went to the despised and rejected, and he was one of them.

One such despised person was Matthew, the tax collector. One day this man was at work in his tollhouse on the overland customs route between Damascus and the Mediterranean. Tax collectors were despised people. To religious Jews they were contaminated men because they worked for Gentiles. Since no respectable Jew would do this, the Roman Government usually recruited its tax collectors from the lower classes of society. And tax collectors were an unscrupulous lot, who overcharged the taxpayers and pocketed the profits themselves.

We do not know that Matthew was a shady character, but neither do we have any reason to think otherwise about him. We only know that he was a man who could hear the gospel while those who despised him were deaf to it. So it was that as one customer turned from the booth with the usual grumbling and oaths, the next one paused and waited for Matthew to look up from counting the change. When he did so, Matthew's eyes met the eyes of Jesus. Jesus said, "Follow me." "And," the record says simply, "he rose and followed him."

Any answer to the great invitation to discipleship has this quick, decisive tone to it. A person may have been thinking about it for years, but "never got around to it." Yet when the decision comes, he makes it because Jesus becomes for him a person whose call cannot be ignored.

The summons to personal discipleship is a summons to church membership. Many people probably question this. "Can't I be a good Christian and not be in the church?" they ask. The reason why discipleship to Jesus Christ is discipleship *in the church* will be discussed in a later chapter. It is enough at this point to say that when Jesus called his disciples to himself, he called them into his church.

ACTING ON THE INVITATION

As one denomination in the universal church of Jesus Christ, The United Presbyterian Church has established a form of church order by which a person can signify his response to Jesus' invitation. The order is based upon Christian doctrine and is an attempt to be faithful to the will of God for decent and orderly practices in his church. It is an order built around the two sacraments of Baptism and the Lord's Supper.

The sacrament of Baptism marks a person's entrance into discipleship in the church. It is given to children of Christian believers because we think it is the will of God that children even from their infancy should be marked as those who are numbered among the people of God. When adults join the church, they are either confirming the vows their parents made for them at their baptism or taking the baptismal vows themselves for the first time (if they were not baptized in infancy).

It is therefore entirely proper to call church membership classes for persons coming on confession of faith "confirmation classes," because most of the persons in such classes will be making their personal response to the invitation for the first time. They are learning what it means to confirm, to take for themselves, the vows taken for them in their baptism.

More generally in The United Presbyterian Church, however, such classes are called "communicants classes," because the technical name for church members is "communicants." This simply means that such members *commune* at the Lord's Table. Those persons who have been baptized, and who profess their faith for themselves, receive the sacrament of the Lord's Supper. When they do this they both witness to something and receive something. They witness to their faith in Jesus Christ, that is, their discipleship, and they receive his power and grace to be faithful disciples.

When you join The United Presbyterian Church, therefore, you become a person, who, having received Baptism, receives the Lord's Supper. There are three ways in which a person can join The United Presbyterian Church. The first is by confession of faith, the second is by letter of transfer from another Christian church, and the third is by reaffirmation of faith. This third method is for those persons who once joined a Christian church but who now, for any one of many reasons, cannot receive a letter of transfer.

The questions asked by the minister on behalf of the session of the church in the last two instances simply require the promise that in this particular church the person will continue in the loyalty to Christ and the church which he affirmed when he first united with a Christian fellowship. This answer becomes a reaffirmation of his first confession.

It is well, therefore, to record here the questions asked a person when he declares his Christian faith for the *first* time, as these questions are given in *The Book of Common Worship:*

*"Question:* Do you confess your faith in God the Father Almighty, Maker of heaven and earth, and in Jesus Christ his only Son our Lord, and do you promise with the aid of the Holy Spirit to be Christ's faithful disciple to your life's end?

*"Answer:* I do.

*"Question:* Do you confirm the vows taken for you in Baptism and with a humble and contrite heart put your whole trust in the mercy of God, which is in Christ Jesus our Lord?

*"Answer:* I do.

*"Question:* Do you promise to make diligent use of the means of grace, to share faithfully in the worship and service of the church, to give of your substance as the Lord may prosper you, and to give your whole heart to the service of Christ and his kingdom throughout the world?

*"Answer:* I do."

These are serious vows, too serious to be answered

lightly or unthinkingly. The rest of this book will help you understand what they mean.

THE CHRISTIAN LIFE

Answering "I do" to these questions is only the first, not the last, response to the great invitation "to be Christ's faithful disciple to your life's end." Each day is a day of discipleship, a day of obedience. The promise "to give your whole heart to the service of Christ and his kingdom throughout the world" is not merely a pious phrase. It implies that in personal conduct and in public decision each Christian will acknowledge Christ's authority over him and try to be obedient to Christ's will. It is a vow more far-reaching than the marriage promise or the acceptance of a professional code of ethics. The person who does not intend to be true to it has not heard Christ's invitation and should not make a promise he knows he will not try to keep.

Discipleship is serious business. It is time now to learn who it is who calls us, why his invitation meets our needs, and what it means to serve him in the church.

The questions are from *The Book of Common Worship*, copyright, 1946, by the Board of Christian Education of the Presbyterian Church in the United States of America.

# CHAPTER 2

# Who, Then, Is Jesus?

If Christianity is a relationship to Jesus Christ, who, then, is Jesus?

A father and his three-year-old son were having a conversation about Jesus. The little boy said, "Let's go see Jesus." Wondering what was coming next out of the fertile imagination of a three-year-old, the father said, "Where shall we go to see him?" "Over in the cemetery," replied the boy.

For a minute the father was nonplussed. Then he remembered that in the cemetery near their home was a statue of Jesus with outstretched arms, and also two mosaics, one of the Good Shepherd and the other of the Last Supper.

This father hopes that in time the child will have a different understanding of Jesus. Seeds for that understanding can be sown now. But many adults today might not have any better answer to the question, "Where shall we find Jesus?" They know that a man by this name once existed, and that he was a very good man. But where is he now? "Over in the cemetery."

The church says something else. It says that Jesus Christ is alive today. Though he was once a real man who lived and died, he rose from the dead. This is a tremendous

17

mystery. Any bona fide answer to the question, "Who, then, is Jesus?" will involve us in this mystery. Our choice is either to ignore the whole record of Jesus' career or to grapple with a mystery.

But if we are interested in what Christianity is all about, we really do not have this option. Our only choice is to confront the record and face what it tells us about Jesus Christ.

As a broad framework for our investigation we shall turn to the Christian experience of a man who said of himself, "For to me to live is Christ." In a brief, lyrical section of his letter to the Philippians, the apostle Paul gives his answer to our question. Here is what he tells us about Jesus:

> "Christ Jesus, who, though he was in the form of God, did not count equality with God a thing to be grasped, but emptied himself, taking the form of a servant, being born in the likeness of men. And being found in human form he humbled himself and became obedient unto death, even death on a cross. Therefore God has highly exalted him and bestowed on him the name which is above every name, that at the name of Jesus every knee should bow, in heaven and on earth and under the earth, and every tongue confess that Jesus Christ is Lord, to the glory of God the Father." *Phil. 2: 5-11.*

## "IN THE FORM OF GOD, . . .
### IN THE LIKENESS OF MEN"

The first time anyone knew Jesus, of course, he was known as a flesh-and-blood person. Jesus was born of a woman in a specific place in Palestine. He lived at a definite time in human history, from the period of one ruler to another, from Herod to Pontius Pilate. He ate and drank, like anyone else. He wept like any other person touched by need and sorrow. He died, the same as we all have to do. He was really a man.

But those persons who knew him most intimately and felt uniquely bound to him came to another conclusion about him. He was not only human. He was also divine. This is the mystery about Jesus, and the entire New Testament is filled with the atmosphere of this mystery: conceived in a woman, born in a stable, yet angels sing at his birth, shepherds are told that he is "Christ the Lord," and a star leads Wise Men to Bethlehem. When he becomes a man, he submits to baptism, yet he is called "the Lamb of God, who takes away the sin of the world!"

He teaches, and people are aware that there is unique authority behind his words. When he heals he does not merely make the sick well, but, on his own authority, forgives their sins—a thing only God can do. Whereas others before him had promised a kingdom, he declares that in him the Kingdom has come. Just before he is to die, he not only predicts what will happen but also announces that he will rise from the dead!

It is impossible to write a purely "human life of Jesus" and do justice to this man. It is equally impossible to write his story as if he had never really lived but was only a remarkable spiritual idea. Whatever you do with Jesus, you have to take both his humanity and deity into equal account. In him God assumed "the likeness of men."

We have to live with that idea a while before we begin to recognize the unexpectedness of it. If, when we stop to think about it, it does not overwhelm us as it should, this is probably because we accommodate it to our reasoning. To hold that Jesus is human and divine then seems to say no more than this: "He was several degrees better than the rest of us, who all have something of the divine spark in us. Man and God are very much akin."

The Jews obviously did not feel that way. Their lofty conception of God made it unthinkable that any man could dare to claim to be divine. Anyone who made that claim was a blasphemer who ought to be killed. (See *John 5: 18*.) This much has to be said for the Pharisees who wanted Jesus crucified—that they wished to preserve what they thought was the honor of God. In the ninth chapter of the Gospel of John there is the story of a blind man healed by Jesus. The man is brought before the Pharisees and told to deny that it was Jesus who healed him. The authorities refuse to recognize Jesus' power. But the man is convinced that the one who healed him had the power of God in him. (*V. 33*.) When Jesus returns and asks him if he believes in the Son of Man, and identifies himself as that Son, the man confesses his faith and worships him. (*Vs. 35-38*.)

What happened here describes how and why men believe that Jesus, who was among them as a man, was in the form of God. There is no other way to account for such a person. When a person finds life, or is able to see, through the power of this man, he knows that here is someone at work who is more than a man. *It is because of what Jesus does that men know he is both God and man.* Obviously, the person who is not aware of anything Christ has done for him does not know him as God and man, even though he may repeat from now to his dying day what the Creed says on this matter.

But when men receive Jesus as Lord, then a creed comes alive. Take the one most familiar in Christendom, the Apostles' Creed. The person who receives Jesus as Lord can divide this Creed under two headings. The first part, beginning with "I believe in God," through ". . . the Holy Ghost," describes "What God has told about himself in Jesus Christ"; and the rest of the Creed can carry the title

"What God has done for us in Jesus Christ." The Creed becomes personal, something for you and me, because it is about a Person.

It was this faith in Jesus which led Paul to speak of him as he does in Philippians: "in the form of God, . . . in the likeness of men." Even more striking is what Paul writes about Jesus in another letter: the Son "is the image of the invisible God, the first-born of all creation; for in him all things were created, in heaven and on earth, visible and invisible, . . . all things were created through him and for him. He is before all things, and in him all things hold together." (*Col. 1:15-17.*) The Gospel of John testifies to the same truth when, calling Jesus "the Word," it says: "In the beginning was the Word, and the Word was with God, and the Word was God. He was in the beginning with God; all things were made through him, and without him was not anything made that was made." (*John 1:1-3.*)

A LIFE OF UTTER OBEDIENCE

But why did God come to man in Jesus? He was born to reconcile men to God. The next chapter will give a fuller explanation of this thought. But the person of Jesus cannot be separated from the work of Jesus. Who he is can be properly understood only in the light of what he came to do. We must at this point, therefore, look at his vocation—what he came to do—for what it can tell us in answer to our question, "Who, then, is Jesus?" For Jesus to be the very person of God in human form meant for him to be the Suffering Servant of God, spoken of so many centuries before in *Isa., ch. 53.*

A servant is "a person at the disposal of another—to carry out his will, do his work, represent his interests." (George Adam Smith.) The perfect servant would be the one who was utterly obedient to the will of his master. In this Jesus was the perfect servant of God, for he was absolutely obedient to his Father and did completely what his Father had sent him into the world to do.

What did God send Jesus to do? He sent him to die on a cross. This was the reason for Jesus' coming to earth. The cross was, therefore, not simply an unjust, cruel, and unexpected end to a remarkably good life. It was not merely one other illustration of the bitter fact of life that, in this kind of world, innocent people often suffer at the hand of malicious men. He was more than a great teacher being martyred for his ideals. Jesus' death was "according to the definite plan and foreknowledge of God," said Peter in his first sermon. (*Acts 2: 23.*) It is possible to say that when God sent his Son to earth he sent him to die.

But why? In order that the gap between God and man might be bridged, in order that man might be reconciled to God, from whom he is an alien and a stranger. This is something that no man can do for himself; it is something only God can do. Therefore, because he was unwilling to allow the gulf to remain, God sent his Son to earth to die.

Men had been servants of God before Jesus, but Jesus' vocation was to be the Suffering Servant in a unique way. His obedience required that he follow through the will of God all the way to the cross, and he was fully obedient. Although other faithful servants have been called upon to suffer, only Jesus suffered for the sake of reconciling men to God.

In his obedience Jesus showed in a thoroughly unmistakable way that "God is love." God reconciles us because he loves us. And God's love is suffering love. From this time on, all human love is judged and defined in the light of this divine love which sent God himself to the cross for our sakes and for our salvation.

Who, then, is Jesus? He is the obedient Son of God, who came to men as the Suffering Servant of God for the sake of their salvation.

THE NAME ABOVE ALL NAMES

After Jesus' death, so the New Testament tells us, he rose from the dead, appeared to men of faith for forty days, and then returned to heaven, the place he had come from. There, Paul says, "God has highly exalted him and bestowed on him the name which is above every name, that at the name of Jesus every knee should bow, in heaven and on earth and under the earth, and every tongue confess that Jesus Christ is Lord, to the glory of God the Father." (*Phil. 2:9-11.*)

In the Old Testament we read of God's saying to his servant Moses, "Man shall not see me and live" (*Ex. 33: 20*). So great is the glory and brilliance of God. But Jesus changes all this. What men could not look upon, he has made known. "He who has seen me has seen the Father," Jesus said. (*John 14:9.*) God is still high and holy, infinitely greater than we, full of majesty, to be held in awe and reverence; but he has also "dwelt among us." We come to God, therefore, not as people who fearfully tremble before a remote and unknowable being, but as people who have seen God in Jesus Christ and who "have boldness and confidence of access through our faith in him" (*Eph. 3:12*).

This is what it means for us to be able to call Jesus "Lord." "Lord" is a name for God. It signifies authority and rule. Jesus is the one who is in authority over our individual wills and consciences. He is in authority over the church. He is in authority over the course of history. He, "fairest Lord Jesus," is "ruler of all nature." And we are his disciples. Christianity is that relationship in which men are permanently bound to Jesus as their Lord.

This Lordship is not fully known by all men. But the purpose for which God has called Christians into the church is that the church may witness to Christ as Lord in such a way that in time men will realize that "the kingdom of the world has become the kingdom of our Lord and of his Christ, and he shall reign for ever and ever" (*Rev. 11:15*). When that comes to pass, *"every* knee" *will* bow before him, and *"every* tongue" will confess that which Christian tongues now confess—"that Jesus Christ is Lord, to the glory of God the Father."

But this witnessing, this confessing of Christ as Lord, is not something that the individual Christian and the church do on their own. Jesus does not sit in solitary grandeur in heaven, watching what is going on in his church, but taking no part in it. When the Christian and the church are faithful in their work of witnessing, they acknowledge that this has been Christ at work in them. "The transcendent power belongs to God and not to us." (*II Cor. 4:7*.) Jesus spoke of this continuing, working power as the power of the Holy Spirit: "He who believes in me will also do the works that I do; and greater works than these will he do, because I go to the Father. . . .

"I will pray the Father, and he will give you another Counselor, to be with you for ever, even the Spirit of truth . . . ; you know him, for he dwells with you, and will be in you.

"I will not leave you desolate; I will come to you" (*John 14:12, 16-18*).

### THE TRINITY

Who, then, is Jesus? A man among men, in coming to the world, he came as the revealer in his own person of God the Father; he came as the Son of God, who gave himself as the Savior of the world; and he is now at work in the world, through the Holy Spirit.

In our services we sing: "Glory be to the Father, and to the Son, and to the Holy Ghost." The Doxology sung in almost all our churches is also an expression of praise to the God who is in three Persons, and the same pattern is to be found in many another hymn. This idea of the Holy Trinity arose not from any formal New Testament teaching on the Trinity as such, but was made necessary by what Scripture says and what Christian experience confirms, for the New Testament speaks of Jesus Christ in such terms as can only be applied to God. Again, it speaks of the Holy Spirit (in older language, the Holy Ghost) so as to show that it is through the Spirit that God in Christ takes possession of us. It is not a case of there being three different gods. There is one God—the Father revealed in Christ our Lord, through the Holy Spirit.

We need but consult the words of Jesus himself: "He who has seen me has seen the Father" (*John 14:9*). Moreover, he assured his disciples that the Father would send the Holy Spirit, in Jesus' name, to "teach you all things, and bring to your remembrance all that I have said to you" (*v. 26*). The experience of knowing Jesus as God's own Son, and being inwardly compelled by the Holy Spirit to call him Lord, is what lies behind our doctrine of the Triune God.

This is one meaning of faith: affirming as true what one knows through experience. Faith has been defined as "betting your life that there is a God." But faith is not an act by which one determines to believe, despite every evidence to the contrary. Christian faith is being grasped (through the Holy Spirit) by the reality that does exist, namely, Jesus Christ, and becoming his disciple. The blind man believed in Jesus because he had experienced the power of Jesus in his own life. Jesus lay hold on him and made him able to see. His act of faith was his commitment to Jesus as the One in whom he found life and light.

So the opposite of faith is not doubt, as is sometimes thought. Faith leaves plenty of room for doubt, because within the relationship of commitment a person can ask all kinds of questions and know they will not change the relationship in which he stands. The opposite of faith is sin, the refusal to receive God as he offers himself to his people in his Son, Jesus Christ. A person does not believe Jesus is the Son of God and then become his disciple. He becomes his disciple and then knows that the one who has called him is God among men. Thus church membership does not begin with the acceptance of a creed. It begins with the acceptance of a Person, and in a creed the church member makes formal affirmation of the belief he knows from experience. That Person is the One of whom the Christian sings, loosening his creed from the bondage of mere words and giving it the cadence of poetry and the sublimity of song:

> "All hail the power of Jesus' Name!
> Let angels prostrate fall;
> Bring forth the royal diadem,
> And crown Him Lord of all."

CHAPTER 3

# Christ the Peacemaker

What does Jesus Christ have to offer you? Why concern yourself about discipleship? Specifically, why belong to the church?

It would be comforting to think that church membership guarantees what everyone seems to be seeking nowadays—"peace of mind." A few years ago streetcars were placarded with signs that read: "Take your troubles to church on Sunday—thousands leave them there." The Bible has a good deal to say about peace in Christ, but there it is called "the peace . . . which passes all understanding." What the Bible calls peace does not mean a formula for being at ease, poised, and self-confident in a tragic and nerve-racking world.

If we are indeed to find peace in Christ, who overcame the world, we shall have to wrestle first with the problems that make his victory significant. We shall have to struggle with the problem of evil, the problem of pain, the question of whether or not life has a purpose, the question of whether or not it matters if life has any purpose. Then, and only then, shall we be able to appreciate Jesus' word of encouragement—"Be of good cheer . . ."

We can never escape from life through refusing to take it seriously.

27

## "HOW LONG, O LORD?"

Here is a young couple with three children, trying to make ends meet. The marital bliss they hoped for has been marred by the continuous struggle to provide shoes for the baby, a new roof for the house, and tires for the car. The husband is worn out with commuting to the job and competing in the office; the wife, by the toil of household chores. If one of the children were killed in an accident, what would they do? Try to keep a stiff upper lip and get by on self-contained courage? What is their philosophy of life? Simply that they are not happy now, but perhaps tomorrow will be better? In the kind of life they lead, can the church *promise* them anything? Can it undertake to deliver "peace of mind"?

Here is a widow whose only son was killed in the war several years ago. Last year her husband died. She is bitter against fate, or against God, or whatever she calls the power that seems to be responsible for her personal calamities. She is lonely; she feels frightened and lost. What can the church offer her in her distress?

On the other hand, there is the business official whom life has treated well. He and his wife are in the best of health, and they are surrounded by good friends. His daughters are happily married. He is secure in his job, and he looks forward to generous retirement benefits. He is satisfied with life as it is and is untroubled by the woes of the world. What does the church offer him that he does not already enjoy?

Then there is the young girl teaching in a school for mentally retarded children. Some of them seem content in their limitations, but others are morose, morbid, divided personalities. She asks: "Why are these selected for such a fate? What have they done to deserve this?" What answer can the church provide in her bitter questioning?

Or look at this man. He has his present job because he subtly undermined the confidence of his superiors in the man who should have had it. His appearance of honest sincerity won him his advancement. But his conscience gives him no quietness, for he knows he has gained his position under false colors. How can the church help him now?

These are some of the people who make up the everyday drama of life. What has Jesus Christ to do with their problems? What can the church say to them that goes beyond a homespun philosophy of life which enables them to get along as best they can? What difference would it really make to any of them if they sought comfort and a new beginning in the church of Christ?

GRACE GIVEN AND RECEIVED

Scripture offers many examples.

In *Luke 7: 36-50* we have the story of a woman who found God in Christ. She was a prostitute—a person completely estranged from God and society. We are not told where she first saw or heard Jesus. We know nothing of any words he may have spoken to her. However, somewhere along the way of life she had met or heard of him. Then one day when he was at a dinner nearby, she entered the house, and, "weeping, she began to wet his feet with her tears, and wiped them with the hair of her head, and kissed his feet, and anointed them with the ointment."

She had found in Christ grace, mercy, kindness, and above all acceptance. In the light of that grace she could see what she had been and cling to the feet of him who pointed to a way out of her moral failure. Now she knew just how lonely she had been, how separated from God and her fellow creatures. Now she could discern why there was no peace for her; now she could perceive the hopelessness in which she had long lived. For the first time, perhaps, she recognized how bitter life had become.

She knew her sin—knew it in the forgiveness offered by Jesus Christ. She knew how far she was from God—knew it when God drew near in grace and love. She knew her willfulness—knew it when the gentleness of Christ overcame her will. Now her will was committed to his. Now she was reconciled to the God whom she had been fighting off for so many years without knowing whom she had opposed, or whence her inner conflicts came.

It was in the house of a Pharisee that this lost-and-found woman created the scene. The Pharisee, as a matter of course, would have expelled her. She had no place in respectable society. At best he might have exhorted her to abandon her wicked ways. It may be surmised, in turn, that the moralistic Pharisee would have had no influence whatsoever on a woman so deeply entrenched in the life she had been living. People are seldom "reformed" by a stern wagging of the finger. Not until she had learned what Jesus' grace was like could she either know her problem or do anything about it.

The Pharisee would have given her short shrift. It is remarkable that the people with whom Jesus, on his part, was least able to get along were the moralistic Pharisees who were so sternly preoccupied with keeping every last detail of the law of God. To Jesus, and to Paul his apostle, God's law was summed up in love. This did not mean taking moral laws lightly, as though sin were of no importance. What it meant was going all out to help persons estranged from God find their way back to him. It meant dying for people, not simply reproving them.

Jesus strongly reproved the Pharisees, because they fought evil with self-righteousness. In the end he died for them too, seeking forgiveness for those who slew him out of their conviction that thereby they did God service. By Jesus' death even a Pharisee might learn that the way to peace with God is not by what we do for ourselves but by what someone else does for us. And even if they did not learn it, the love was still there for the taking. The love that alone could reconcile a man to God was poured forth for all men and for all time to come.

## THE HEART TURNED INSIDE OUT

The secret of man's unhappiness is his separation from God. Man may not know it. He may attribute his misery to almost everything but this. When, however, he discovers God in His *graciousness,* he discovers also the source of his own troubles. What it is like to be close to God brings to light the unhappiness of being far from him— what Paul calls "having no hope and without God in the world."

This joyful finding of the difference between being close to or far from God also explains another mystery of life. Who has not wondered why men, who could be so much happier living in peace with other men, perversely insist on doing harm to their fellows? The answer to this age-old riddle is that we are all separated from God, and therefore frustrated more deeply than we know; and since we cannot take out our frustration on God, we turn on our fellow men. Uneasy in our hearts about our strained relationships with our Creator, we give ourselves over to self-seeking—at the expense of others.

Only in one great moment did man become what he was meant to be. When Jesus died—in absolute obedience to his Father's will, which meant absolute love toward others —then and there humanity lived up to what God expected of it. In that moment the perfect Man bore the whole weight of misery which this world's separation from God imposes, crying out, "My God, my God, why hast thou forsaken me?" He was alienated from God, however, not on account of his own sins but on account of ours. This was the love which made his sacrifice meaningful. He had lived *for us,* not for himself. Thus he could immediately add from the cross, "It is finished." From his living and his dying a fountain of new life would spring up for those who henceforth should be swept along in this fresh stream. It was a new beginning for mankind, and since that day on Calvary human history has never been the same as it was before. *Jesus brought God and man together,* desiring to end the ancient history of man's lonely, self-willed, angry separation from his Maker.

It is in this sense that Christ is our peace. In one momentous event he changed the relationship between God and his people. The word for it is "reconciliation." What the church offers, then, is not a bag of psychological tricks to make people feel better about a world all too full of sin and woe. It offers the knowledge that through Christ Jesus there is a new and living way to be at peace with God—a result of which may be peace within our minds in so far as we lay hold on what *Christ* is, rather than on some supposed capacities inside ourselves.

Because of this joyful message, the church can also claim to set men's feet on a path that will lead them to peace with one another. The barriers between man and man fall down when the barrier between God and man dissolves. Now we need not try to live by ourselves, or for ourselves, in sheer self-defense, as if there were no God and no neighbor in our lives. Living for God, we can live for one another. Luther taught that sin springs from *the heart curved in upon itself.* What manner of sin is there that does not answer to this description? The overcoming of sin thus means turning outward from ourselves toward God and other people.

## WHAT OF US?

But what about the people we described earlier? What does reconciliation in Christ mean to the frantic young couple caught in today's hectic living, to the bitter widow, to the happy and secure businessman, to the sensitive teacher who is disturbed by the suffering there is in the world, to the man who has cheated in his business?

As long as they are not found by Jesus Christ, nothing will change for them. They will continue to live "lives of quiet desperation," of unreconciled bitterness, or of self-satisfaction. Finding it impossible to make any sense out of the jumbled universe, sensitive people will simply stop asking questions to which they can discover no answer.

But if they are open to the Word of God in Christ, the pieces of the puzzle may begin to fall into place. They will face realistically the human predicament—which is separation and disappointment and frustration and anxiety. More salary will not change the young parents' problems. Nothing can restore to the widow her dead son. The war in which he lost his life is part of the sin of a separated world. The secure older couple may discern that they have not been sensitive enough to the problems of other people. The teacher will recognize that some children in her school are victims of disorders of nature and others are victims of the sins of their parents. The businessman will see that there is no justification for the wrong that he did. And all the people will come to realize that within each of them is that inward alienation which makes this a separated, disordered world. All of them need to hear that for this condition there is the promise of healing.

This is the beginning of the return of health. In that hour—the hour of hearing the promise—they are close to their own reconciliation. It remains for them to see what this act of God means for them in their particular needs. In all likelihood the situation will not change dramatically. The house will still need its new roof, the job will still exert its pressures, but the family can be released from its self-centeredness and from the futility of seeing nothing in view but the next problem. Having cut themselves off from God, they could not see beyond tomorrow; but being reconciled to God, they find themselves caught up in his eternal purpose and love.

The fortunate couple can be led to realize that their prosperity has stood between them and God. In their ease and security and satisfaction, they have not looked beyond their own happiness to feel concerned about the unhappiness of others. Reconciliation awakens in them this holy concern.

We could go on to imagine what the reconciling gospel might mean to the other hypothetical instances we have described, but that is not necessary. The thing every man has to learn is that though he is part of a world that is alienated from God, God wills his reconciliation. He reconciles a man by speaking this one strong word to him, *"You are accepted!"* God does not ask us to become more morally righteous before we come to him, or to present him with an impressive balance sheet of the good that we have done which we vainly think will outweigh the evil that is in us. Our reunion with him is not achieved through bargaining. It comes only as faith speaks the joyful, releasing word to us—"You are accepted!" The summary of what Christianity is all about, why Jesus came, is this: "God was in Christ reconciling the world to himself, not counting their trespasses against them" (*II Cor. 5:19*).

WHAT NEXT?

This word of acceptance and reconciliation is the clue to all that Jesus taught. It is what the gospel is about.

Whether we hear of "the Kingdom of God," or "eternal life," or "new life in Christ," we know that the New Testament is speaking of the life a man lives when he learns of his acceptance through the work of Christ.

The earliest Gospel ushers us quickly into the preaching of Jesus, and gives us his first words: "The time is fulfilled, and the kingdom of God is at hand; repent, and believe in the gospel" (*Mark 1: 15*). That is what, in effect, the prostitute heard him say. God's Kingdom, so to speak, was rushing in upon her. The long-expected break-through of God into human life had now happened. She could now, in this moment, learn that she was reconciled to God. What she needed to do was to acknowledge that she needed reconciliation, that she was alienated ("repent"). And she knew what it meant to repent, because she had heard that her reconciliation had already taken place ("believe in the gospel"). Though she could not describe it that precisely, her tears of joy and thankfulness showed that she knew what it meant to be accepted by her Lord.

The Gospel According to John puts it this way: "For God so loved the world that he gave his only Son, that whoever believes in him should not perish but have eternal life. For God sent the Son into the world, not to condemn the world, but that the world might be saved through him" (*John 3: 16-17*). This says the same thing as the verse from Mark's Gospel, adding these significant notes: *God wills* the reconciliation ("loves") of all men (although it is given only to those who believe); and Jesus came not to condemn but to reconcile ("save"). This saying suggests that men do not need to be reminded of their separation and alienation. They are only too well aware of it. What they need to hear is that *they can be saved*.

There are times, however, when men need to be made aware that they are separated from God and must recognize the moral responsibility in their sin. Here Paul speaks with telling force, though with no less awareness of grace than Jesus or John. The contrast he describes is between the old being and the new. Before a man knows Christ, says Paul, he lives under the frustration of seeking salvation by obedience to laws and never finding it. In such a condition he cries: "Wretched man that I am! Who will deliver me from this body of death?" ( *Rom. 7: 24*). In this condition one is not merely alienated. Life is as hopeless and futile as death. But the way to come to new life is to die to the old creature and become a new man! This is Paul's graphic way of describing the experience of faith and repentance. "We were buried therefore with him by baptism into death, so that as Christ was raised from the dead by the glory of the Father, we too might walk in newness of life." (*Ch. 6: 4*.) The Christian change-over from separation to reconciliation is a process of death and resurrection.

THE NEW LIFE OF THE KINGDOM

What are the characteristics of this new life? The chief characteristic is that the Christian lives by grace (forgiveness) and walks by faith (in the power of the One who has saved him). One description of the new life is what is usually called the Sermon on the Mount (*Matt., chs. 5 to 7*). As long as these chapters are taken to describe a life that any man ought to be able to achieve, if he does the best he can, they become impossible ideals, impracticable for this world. Just "doing the best we can" is the very thing that shuts us off from God. But when these sayings of Jesus are seen as representing the kind of life the *reconciled* man will lead—by Christ's grace and not by his own power—they must be taken seriously. This is how our Lord lived.

Jesus said, for example, "Blessed are the peacemakers, for they shall be called sons of God." This is not merely praise for umpires and arbitrators. To make peace is to reconcile and be reconciled. The distinctive mark of the Christian man is that he is reconciled. The distinctive act of the Christian, then, is that he seeks to reconcile. He finds reconciliation within himself through the word of forgiveness, and in forgiveness he seeks reconciliation with his alienated neighbor. Christ, who made peace between ourselves and God, when we were strangers, asks us by his grace to make peace near and far upon earth.

To be in Christ means to be accepted. It means, then, to accept others, as God for Jesus' sake has accepted us. This is the beginning of the Christian life in the church of Christ.

# CHAPTER 4

# "The True and Lively Word"

How does a person know that he is accepted by God, reconciled to him, called to live with him in the fellowship of the Kingdom?

Recall the woman who came to Jesus and anointed him in gratitude because she knew the truth of the word, "You are accepted!" *How* did she know? Because she heard Jesus speak the good news of salvation, and it was to her ears a word addressed directly and personally to her.

A person begins this Christian life when he hears this same word and receives it in this same way. Today, since Jesus is not among men in the flesh, he speaks to men by the Holy Spirit. The Spirit reveals to a man his need to be reconciled, awakens in him the faith that Jesus is his reconciler, and leads him to receive the gift of his acceptance. This same Spirit calls a man into the fellowship of the church, and throughout his Christian life helps him to see his Christian responsibilities and strengthens him to be faithful to them.

How does the Holy Spirit speak to a man? The Roman Catholic Church declares that the Holy Spirit speaks to men only through the church and its doctrine. But Protestants cannot agree. It is the historic position of Protestantism that the Spirit speaks to men through the Bible.

Though the church is essential for the Christian experience, the church is to be obeyed only in so far as it is faithful to this Word spoken through Scripture.

It is because the Holy Spirit speaks through the Bible that an ancient prayer refers to Scripture as "the true and lively Word." When the Holy Spirit speaks through the Bible, the Word of God becomes a living reality. Scripture comes alive. And we come alive, as the Scripture becomes God's Word to us, to awaken faith in us or to direct us in the way we should walk.

THE AUTHORITY OF THE BIBLE

It is hard to know how people regard the Bible today. Most people would agree that it is a unique and unusual book; many people would admit that they should read it more than they do; but probably a good number of very sincere Christians wonder just what authority it is supposed to have over their faith and their daily living. We live today in the backwash of the unfortunate nineteenth-century conflict between science and religion, and there are probably a large number of people whose faith in the Bible has been shaken by the supposed contradictions between the Bible record and scientific facts.

This uneasiness can be a good thing. It has always been wrong to make the Bible something it is not. To think that God set out in the Bible to provide for all time a precise description of scientific phenomena is to misunderstand completely what the Bible is about and why it was written. The Bible is not a scientific textbook. It is the record of God's relationship to man and man's relationship to God. It is a good thing if people can be led to ask questions about Biblical authority in order to discover the real meaning of Scripture.

A simple little religious ditty which most children of

the church school know poses this matter of the authority
of the Bible in a vivid way. The children sing:

> "Jesus loves me! this I know,
> For the Bible tells me so."

It is profoundly true that the Bible is the place in which
God's love for us is made known. But how do we know
that this record is true, that God really does love us? Because the Holy Spirit makes the gospel of love something
"true and lively" for us. *He* tells us what is in the Bible,
and the Bible does not speak without him.

The Christian's authority is not the Bible *as a book*. The
Christian's authority is Jesus Christ, who comes to man
today in the Holy Spirit, speaking through Scripture. The
Bible has authority because it puts Christ in authority
over us.

But of course there is no other place in which Christ is
made known to men. Nature, by itself, cannot bring us to
Christ. He is not revealed—really made known—by the
proofs of philosophers. As we have seen, it defies reason
that God should become man. In the Bible God reveals
himself to us in Jesus Christ, as that revelation is received
in our hearts by faith through the Holy Spirit. Nothing
else does this. We have to study the Bible if we are to hear
the reconciling word and if we are to live and grow as
Christians. But its authority over us is not the authority
*of a book*. It is not a so-called "paper pope." Its authority
lies in the fact that through it *God* speaks to us, as his
Spirit opens our ears and enlightens our minds.

Because God speaks to men through Scripture, it is
necessary to discover just what Scripture has to say. For
this purpose we ought to use the insights of Biblical schol-
ars who can help us understand the background against
which the Bible was written. This enables us to hear its

message as it was delivered to the people who heard the message for the first time. When light is shed on the historical setting of Bible passages, this is illuminating not only to the scholar, but to the church as a whole and to the individual Christian who is seeking to learn what Scripture means. Through Bible study, words spoken or written long ago become meaningful to us today.

THE UNITY OF THE BIBLE

But how do we go about studying the Bible? Let us imagine a person who is trying to do that for the first time.

He is confronted first of all with a book that is in two uneven sections. What is called the Old Testament is about three fourths of the book. As he begins to read it, it sounds like ancient history. It is interesting, even exciting —but what has this to do with us today? Since it consists of many different kinds of literature—poetry, drama, history, prophecy—it is not surprising if the new reader feels confused. Particular sections will strike fire and give him some sense that here is something important, but he is not quite sure what it is.

Then he turns to the New Testament. He will probably find this more interesting, for the story of Jesus carries an inner fire which attracts even the most casual reader. Yet he has many questions; and should he happen upon the verse in The Acts, "Do you understand what you are reading?" (*Acts 8: 30*), he would look up and say: "Frankly, no. What is this all about?"

Now this particular incident happens to be an excellent place at which to begin opening up the Scripture. The Ethiopian was reading from what is now an Old Testament book, the prophecy of Isaiah, and his instructor, Philip, began with that Scripture to tell him "the good news of Jesus." The significance of Jesus was explained in terms of an Old Testament text. No other single story in the Bible better demonstrates the unity of the Bible.

Jesus came at the end of a long period of preparation for his coming. The Old Testament describes that time of preparation. We cannot properly understand his significance without first understanding what God had done for man before he came in Christ.

Jesus also spoke and taught as a Jew. Though his teaching is universal, much of what he said becomes clear only against its Jewish background.

Jesus' first followers were Jews. They wrote and spoke to Jews. Most of their readers knew what we call the Old Testament, and if we are to comprehend Matthew, Paul, or the writer of the letter to the Hebrews, we must become familiar with the Scripture they drew upon so extensively.

Fundamentally, however, the reader of the Bible must see that, despite its diversity of form, the Word of God tells one story. It is the story of God's grace toward sinful men. The Old Testament describes not just the history of the Jews but man's basic need and God's way of meeting that need. When read in the light of the gospel, God speaks from this section of his book as clearly and decisively as from the New Testament.

### THE BIBLE AND THE CHURCH

The Bible exists so that the church can witness to Jesus Christ. These first Christians were Jews and therefore, as we have seen, they found their Jewish Scriptures (our Old Testament) essential for declaring the gospel to men. (Such a reference as *II Tim. 3:15,* which refers to the Jewish Scriptures, shows the high regard in which the Old Testament was held by the early Christian church.) In the course of church life, letters were written to churches and to individual Christians by men like Paul and Peter, and later the books now called Gospels were composed "that you may know the truth concerning the things of which you have been informed" (*Luke 1:4*). Eventually the church gave these letters, the Gospels, a history called The Acts of the Apostles, and a visionary writing called Revelation, the same status as the Jewish Scriptures, because they recognized that through them God was declaring his will and his way in Jesus Christ. This whole body of writing was regarded as uniquely inspired by God, in a way that no other writings before or since are inspired, because of its witness to Jesus Christ. In making this decision about them, the church was led by the Holy Spirit, acting through the historic church. From that time on few people have seriously doubted that the church was so guided.

To the church is committed the preservation of the Word and the faithful declaring of it. Under this commission the church considers it essential to translate the Bible into the speech of the people in every generation, though as Protestants it will not presume to say that any translation is perfect or authoritative. Under this commission the church considers that its chief function in the world is to teach this Word and preach it, in order that men may come face to face with the Lord who is made known in it.

The function of the Bible and of the church is, therefore, an evangelistic and missionary function. "These are written," declared the writer of the Fourth Gospel—and we today would add "these are translated, taught, and preached"—"that you may believe that Jesus is the Christ, the Son of God, and that believing you may have life in his name" (*John 20:31*). The church does not concentrate on the Bible in order that it might be a select, exclusive group of persons who know a mystery no one else may know. It studies the Bible "that the world may know" that God has sent his Son to all mankind to reveal his love and to bring all men under the sway of his love. (See *John 17:23*).

# CHAPTER 5

# Christ and His Church

The English Congregationalist, P. T. Forsyth, in his book *The Church and the Sacraments,* writes: "The same act which sets us in Christ sets us also in the society of Christ. . . . To be in Christ is in the same act to be in the church." What this says is simply that if you are a Christian you have to be in the church. Add to this the statement from the Westminster Confession of Faith (one of the doctrinal standards of the Presbyterian Church): "The visible church, . . . out of which there is no ordinary possibility of salvation." (Ch. XXV, Sec. 2.) This is a concept of the church which is startling, if not even offensive, to modern Protestants.

It is startling to modern American Protestants for several reasons. One is that most of us do not really know what the church is. We think of the individual church that we know in our community and wonder why *this,* with all its sinfulness, is essential to our Christian commitment.

Therefore, let us ask ourselves, "What is the church?"

## IN CHRIST, IN THE CHURCH

What does it mean to be "in Christ"? This is a characteristic phrase of the New Testament, found most frequently in the letters of the apostle Paul. What it means is that *a*

*Christian is in the disciple-Lord relationship to Jesus Christ.* This is what we have been talking about all along in this book: to be a Christian is to be a disciple of Jesus Christ. A Christian is a person in a new world, the world of Christ's Lordship over his decisions and his life. Jesus called that world the Kingdom of God. So that while the Christian lives and works in the world of making a living, acting as a responsible citizen, being a member of a family, he is simultaneously a citizen of God's Kingdom. Ideally, the decisions and conduct of the world of human relationships are determined by the relationship to Christ in the divine Kingdom; but this is only ideally. Actually, other factors often influence our living more intensively than does our allegiance to our Lord. This is why we pray, "Thy kingdom come, thy will be done, on earth as it is in heaven." But as Christians we are in the Kingdom, though the Kingdom (or perhaps it would be better to say the King) is not fully in us.

We are in the Kingdom as a result of Christ's call, his laying his finger upon us and choosing us as his disciples. We hear this call and answer it in an act of faith.

All of this we have said in the previous chapters. But what relationship has this personal decision to church membership? According to Forsyth, the call in which Christ chooses us to be his disciples is simultaneously the call to be in the church. They are one and the same call, one and the same act. When Christ calls a man, he calls him into the church. If the call to be a disciple does not include also the call to be in the church, one has not truly heard Christ's call.

Why is this so? Because the church is the body of Christ. In one respect this term is a metaphor, conveying the idea that the work of Christ is done in the world as all the members of the church co-ordinate their efforts and perform

their individual functions properly, the same way hands
and feet do the work of the human body. But in a deeper
sense it is more than a figure of speech. Christians are in-
extricably bound to one another because of their common
bond of loyalty to Jesus Christ. They are the body of which
Christ is the head. And in the church all Christians are
one. The distinctions of race, sex, and ability mean nothing so far as their Christian commitment is concerned. We
are all the same—sinners who have found their forgiveness
in Christ, aliens who have been rescued from their separation, foreigners who are now one people. There are differ-
ences of functions among members, but beneath these
distinctions we are one people—the people bound to one
another because we are bound to Jesus Christ.

When we realize that this is what the church is, other
matters fall into line. No particular church has a monopoly
on being bound to Christ. When you join the church of
Christ—on which the Holy Spirit came at Pentecost and
which will exist to eternity—you are one with Episcopa-
lians, Baptists, and the whole company of Christ's people.
The church as we see it on earth seems greatly divided into
denominations, sects, and cults. To the extent that these
divisions obscure the fundamental unity of his church,
they are an offense to God. But for the Christian who is
conscious of what it means to be in the church, these differ-
ences are overcome. He knows that nothing can destroy
the church; Christ has promised that "the gates of hell
shall not prevail against it" (*Matt. 16:18,* KJV).

Nor is any one church the only true church. Such a
claim undermines the concept of what it means to be the
church of Jesus Christ. For it is Christ who matters, and
the church is *true* to the extent that it brings men into relationship with him. To say that any one sect or denomination has a monopoly on this kind of truth is to take

power away from the Holy Trinity and vest it in a particular form of church organization or doctrine. Men cannot ultimately say who is in the church and who is out of it; that is something known only to God.

SIN IN THE CHURCH

People will still ask the question, however, "How do you account for the sinfulness and imperfections of the church?" How can *the body of Christ* possibly be as imperfect as the church and its members obviously are?

No thoughtful Christian can brush off such a question. There have been throughout our history many sincere and serious attempts to answer it. Roman Catholicism, for example, answers it with the teaching that when the voice of the church speaks on matters of doctrine it must be believed, it exercises discipline, it must be obeyed: it is infallible on matters of faith and morals. The pope, when he speaks *ex cathedra,* does not err.

Of course, this answer cannot satisfy Protestant Christians. We cannot concede that any human being, however saintly he may be, or any group of Christians, possesses the infallibility that belongs to Christ alone. Nor can we eliminate for any man his right of private judgment and individual decision. Protestantism has to make the hard choice of living in tension, of recognizing that the church on earth is sometimes more, sometimes less, purely the body of Christ.

In many of its decisions the church has expressed the mind of Christ and been faithful to its calling. But complete faithfulness awaits the time when, at his coming again, the church will be his perfect body—"the fullness of him who fills all in all."

Therefore, we recognize and accept—even though we mourn over—the incompleteness of the church. "The purest churches under heaven are subject both to mixture and error," says the Westminster Confession of Faith; "and some have so degenerated as to become no churches of Christ, but synagogues of Satan. Nevertheless, there shall always be a church on earth, to worship God according to his will." (Ch. XXV, Sec. 5.)

This means that the church always needs to be reformed; reformation never ends, so long as time and sin remain. And reformation is the work of God, using human instruments for that purpose. Man, though a sinner, can be enlightened by God to recognize and correct error and evil. If he can do this in his own life, he can certainly do it in the church and in society. In the process he will give a great deal of weight to the judgments of other Christians; but even the councils of the church can be wrong. Each man, under the discipline of the Word of God, has to distinguish what is right and what is wrong.

Obviously, therefore, one ought not to expect that when he comes into the church he will be entering a fellowship of perfect men or that he will suddenly become perfect himself on the day he publicly professes his faith in Christ. Redemption in Christ is not a guarantee that a man will never sin again, but that when he sins he has "an advocate with the Father, Jesus Christ the righteous; and he is the expiation for our sins . . ." (*I John 2: 1-2*). The church is not a community that needs no forgiveness, but one that needs forgiveness every day. If we were *not* sinful, we would no longer have any need of Jesus Christ. If we were *not* sinful, there would be no reason for the church. For the church is the fellowship of lost persons found by Jesus Christ.

"To be in Christ is in the same act to be in the church." Outside the church "there is no ordinary possibility of salvation." These statements reflect both a word of Jesus,

"I will build my church," and a word of Paul, "Christ loved the church." It is a great and sobering thing to be called to be a Christian; it is equally magnificent and serious to be called into the church, the body of Christ. Christ has condescended to be the head of this body, our head, our Lord; and he has not left us alone. We are united to him, and we are united with one another in him. This is the framework in which we live Christian lives.

# PART II

*Presbyterian Background and Practice*

CHAPTER 6

# The Risk in Being United Presbyterian

What is distinctive about being a United Presbyterian? In a way, this is a wicked question. It is part of the perversity of human nature that people enjoy being different from anyone else. If we try too hard to make out that The United Presbyterian Church is unlike every other Christian body, we shall end up by transforming ourselves into a sect. The mark of a sect is that it is peculiar, and, in its own estimate, in possession of absolute truth. It views itself as so superior to all other people that it can have little or nothing to do with the rest of Christendom.

It is dangerous, therefore, to look in Presbyterianism for odd doctrines or a superior form of government, at the expense of other Protestant Christians with whom we want to draw a comparison. We are at one with almost all Protestant churches in the great doctrines of Christian faith that have been stated in the first part of this book.

On the whole, it is better to avoid invidious comparisons. If there is anything "peculiar" about us, let others tell us of it! It may not be to our credit. History, however, may give an insight into the nature of the heritage that we claim as Presbyterian. Through history we may learn what Presbyterianism has stood for and what it must stand for today.

REFORMERS ON THE BATTLELINE

It was in the year 1517 that Luther began his revolt against the abuses of the Roman Church. At that time a French boy named John Calvin was eight years old. By the time Calvin had grown to young manhood, the Protestant Reformation was in full swing. Calvin was attracted by Protestant teaching. Above all, he was overwhelmed by the sense of the majesty and sovereignty of God. Scholarly by nature, sickly in body, Calvin found himself led by the very finger of God into what was to be a career highlighted with drama. While still in his youth, Calvin identified himself with the Protestant faith in France, and that fact alone spelled the end of his career as an intellectual in his native country. But also, while still young, Calvin wrote the first edition of what to this day remains one of the greatest of all theological books—*Institutes of the Christian Religion*. This achievement ensured for him both a bad name in Roman Catholic France and a great name in Protestant circles.

So hostile was France to church reformers that Calvin was forced to flee the country. Looking forward to a career as a Protestant scholar, he traveled one day through Geneva, Switzerland, where he expected to stay overnight. This was in 1536. Except for three years of exile from the city, he remained there until his death in 1564. Reformation had already begun in Switzerland, starting with the work of Zwingli, a contemporary of Luther. Geneva itself had but lately revolted against Roman dominance; and it was a pastor of Geneva, William Farel, who persuaded Calvin to stay and help with the thankless task of reorganizing the church in that place.

Had Calvin been able to anticipate in detail all the bitterness of the struggles facing him in the years to follow, he could scarcely have been more unwilling to face the Geneva situation. The city was in disorder. Many motives besides pure religion had contributed to the revolt against Rome, and many of the people desired not so much a Reformed church as freedom from every kind of restraint. Yet, confronted by Farel's challenge, Calvin knew that he had no choice.

The conflict that ensued was fully as bad as he expected. Contending with loose morals and unscrupulous politics in Geneva, both Calvin and Farel were presently expelled by the city government. Yet, when the call to return came three years after his expulsion, Calvin again recognized the impossibility of rejecting the voice of God. He knew that there could be no safe haven where he might escape the responsibilities that God himself had laid upon him. Even though he had been urged to return to Geneva, he was forced to endure political opposition after coming back—opposition even to the point of terrorism. Yet, although by nature a timid man in ill health, he prevailed in most things against his opponents, and under his influence Geneva became a kind of model city of the Reformation. To it came refugees from all parts of Europe; and they carried away with them the ideas learned from Calvin's theological teaching, and from his system of church and civil government. The technical name for this whole school of thought is "Reformed"; and "Reformed Church" is a wider and more descriptive term than "Presbyterianism," for it includes our sister churches, within the same general family, on the Continent of Europe and elsewhere.

Among the refugees who fled for a while to Geneva was the Scottish Reformer, John Knox. Already he had suffered for his faith, having spent many months of agony as a prisoner forced to serve in the French galleys. When he left Geneva to go back to Scotland, he was prepared to organize a church according to a pattern similar to that of Calvin's system. But the remainder of his life, too, was given over to conflict. The support he rallied for a time was soon offset by the crowning of the famed Mary, Queen of Scots—a resourceful and determined woman, whose heart was set upon bringing Scotland back into the Roman Catholic fold. Knox defied her to her face and denounced her whole regime. Eventually her follies brought about her downfall, and the Church of Scotland (Presbyterian) was firmly established.

Meanwhile, Calvin's influence was being felt in widespread fashion. Reformed churches developed in France, Holland, even in Lutheran Germany. Reformed theology deeply influenced the thinking of those who formulated the doctrines held by the Church of England. Even more strongly did it influence those who opposed the policies of the Church of England. These opponents were the Puritans: some of them Presbyterian in outlook, some of them favoring a Congregational system of government, but most of them holding to the basic principles of Reformed theology. In the seventeenth century England was thrown into civil war: a war in which one of the major issues was the effort of the king to enforce the policies of "High Church" Anglican leadership. The Puritans won the war, and the king, Charles I, was beheaded. Although the Presbyterians were not a party to the king's execution, they seized the opportunity to try to make England Presbyterian. It was during this period that the Westminster Assembly was held (1645-1657), from which came our Confession of Faith (today only slightly changed from the original), and the Larger and Shorter Catechisms, which are the basic documents of English-speaking Presbyterianism.

Earlier in the seventeenth century some of the Puritans

had gone to New England, there to set up Congregationalist churches and to advance Calvinist theology. Later,
Presbyterians began to emigrate to the New World; and in
1706 the first presbytery in America was organized around
Philadelphia. As the eighteenth century progressed, Presbyterians in the American settlements increased in both
numbers and vigor. Many of them became ardent sup-
porters of the American Revolution. John Witherspoon,
a Presbyterian minister, was the only clergyman to sign
the Declaration of Independence; and he was appropri-
ately the Moderator of the first General Assembly to be
held on the American continent.

## THEOLOGY IN ACTION

In even so brief a sketch of the beginning and spread
of the Reformed churches, one thing is clear from the simple stating of the facts: Reformed theology was from the
outset aggressive—so much so that this *aggressiveness* might
be taken historically as the hallmark of Presbyterianism.
It is as significant as it is striking that the scholarly Calvin,
who got his reputation through the writing of a book,
proved himself an exceptionally capable man of action.
He never held any government position, yet he dominated
the city of Geneva. Wishing for anything but this kind
of turbulent career, he held to his course and attained his
goal. Knox was such a man as could personally defy a
queen, when monarchs still were believed to rule by divine right. Knox, too, achieved his aim, but not without
struggle. In England, Calvinists overthrew a king. In the
New World, they endured the hardships of pioneering so
that they might have a church that answered to their principles. When the time came for revolt against British
power, Calvinists were in the forefront of the battle for
liberty.

What was the secret of this historic aggressiveness? It was, above all, the sense of the dominance of God. What he called for, men must do. Added to this was clarity of thought. The clear, hard logic of Calvin's theology forced men into action. Calvinists knew neither fuzzy-mindedness nor faintheartedness. Because they thought clearly, they could act decisively. The *Institutes of the Christian Religion* was written by a man who was driven on by the fear of God. Likewise, political as well as church history was made by men compelled by no less a fear. The fear of God and the love of God are to the Christian the same thing: and fearing and loving the sovereign Lord, Calvinists walked the way pointed out to them by God's own finger. Clarity of thought usually means orderliness of thought; and Calvinism was no exception. What Calvin perceived so definitely, he organized into a system of doctrine and of church government that left no loopholes for the slovenly mind. Theology was not poetic fantasy, but the forthright and well-ordered statement of what was believed to be the truth. Within this order men could proceed logically to reach the goal which they felt on each and every occasion that God himself had set before them.

The sense of the leading of God's hand gives us the clue to the famous Calvinistic interest in predestination. Usually people either rejoice in this doctrine or feel embarrassed by it. In the roughest terms, Calvinism has interpreted predestination to mean that God by an eternal decree has designed that some men should be saved and some should be damned. The embarrassment springs from the fact that Calvin and his followers pressed the *negative* side of this doctrine to the extreme, insisting that the counterpart of God's ordaining of some to salvation is naturally a fore-ordination of others to everlasting death. In our own church there is no need any longer to hold to this negative view, for in a declaratory statement appended to the Confession of Faith, in 1903, our church asserted that the doctrine of predestination is to be held in harmony with the doctrine of God's love toward all mankind and his desire that none should perish.

Calvin did not invent the doctrine of predestination—others had taught it, just as strongly, long before his time. If he stressed it in a way that some have thought excessive, it is because he was conscious all his days that God had a destiny for him to fulfill—and woe betide him if he deviated from God's purposes in any and every sphere of action! Throughout the history of the Reformed churches, this sense of a purpose transcending any human purpose has prevailed over the wills of men. So far from Calvinistic predestination being a kind of "fatalism," it has led men on into aggressive and dynamic activity throughout the history of our church. Whatever may be said about the formulation of the doctrine as such, either in Calvin's writing or in our Confession of Faith, it has in history had the very opposite effect of what might have been expected. That is to say, Reformed churchmen did not surrender themselves to blind fate, as though they were playing with a deck of stacked cards, but on the contrary rose up and took action precisely because they believed they were taking their orders from God himself.

To those of the Reformed churches, a confession of faith is not merely an academic statement of what one thinks. It is a public profession of belief, hurled out into the face of unbelief and error. It is, moreover, a profession of belief that cries out to be translated into action. It involves risk—risk of misunderstanding, risk of conflict, risk of suffering, risk of failure. And though the history of the Reformed churches shines with many a dynamic success, there have been failures too. Can we say that failures may not also be dynamic? In France, during the century of the Reformation, the Reformed Church was all but destroyed; and it exists in that country today only as a tiny minority. But the history of the Reformed Church in France, though it does not shine with outward achievement, is brilliant with the blood of martyrs. For the sovereign God is to be obeyed, even at the cost of life itself. Jesus said, "He who loses his life for my sake shall find it."

BEYOND PRESBYTERIANISM

This quality of total allegiance to a sovereign God, expressed in clear theology and aggressive action, is what we may especially cherish as Presbyterians. But in so doing we must pause to remember that this quality can descend to mere human arrogance when it is *our* strength of will rather than God's will that is in the spotlight. Moreover, Presbyterians have no monopoly of courage, steadfastness, or sacrifice. In May, 1934, a group of Reformed churchmen and Lutherans joined, at Barmen, Germany, in a confession (declaration) of faith. In this confession they not only reaffirmed their fundamental beliefs: they explicitly denounced the doctrines of Hitlerism. Thus was born what is know as the "Confessional Church" of Germany— a minority of Christians who stood fast, and many of whom were imprisoned or put to death.

This emergence of a "Confessional Church" in a period of national crisis illustrates in modern times what the Reformers meant by making a confession of faith. It also illustrates how the Protestant faith, clearly understood and stated, can and does cross denominational lines. This, too, is characteristic of historic Calvinism. Calvin's thought, writing, and activity sparked some of the most vigorous developments of the Reformation. Yet there is little in his writing that is original in the sense that some wholly new principle was being proposed. Calvin organized his thought clearly, saw clearly how it applied to actual situations, and then took appropriate action. But he formed no distinctive *sect,* with peculiar ideas all its own. On the contrary, his intention was to gather and systematize what he understood to be the sum of Christian truth for the sake of the whole church of Jesus Christ. For that reason his influence was felt, and continues to be felt, far beyond the borders of those churches which in the technical sense are called "Reformed" or "Presbyterian." For that reason, too, Calvin's thought so influenced so many other churches that we find more than a trace of it in most denominations with which we are likely to be familiar. Without for a moment compromising his views, or indulging in double talk that could mean anything or nothing, through his theology he fashioned a church that was somehow bigger than itself.

The distinctive thing about the Presbyterian tradition, one might almost say, is its very breadth. Nowadays we are hearing much about the ecumenical church, meaning the universal, all-embracing church. In the scope of its theology and the range of its actions, The United Presbyterian Church seeks to be ecumenical. It is ready to take its place in the universal church of Jesus Christ. To stop short of that, to make of Presbyterianism something peculiar and sectarian, is to be un-Presbyterian. Calvin's own wish was very different. He said, "Would that the union between all Christ's churches upon earth were such, that the angels in heaven might join their song of praise."

# CHAPTER 7

# Why We Worship as We Do

Many and various are the activities of the average congregation. The bulletin of almost any active church of
typical size will list an abundance of organizations, with
their times and meeting places. This, it would appear, is
the "practical" side of congregational life, in which everyone gets a chance to participate.

So great is our respect for the value of such meetings,
societies, and special campaigns, that we are apt to resent
the claim that, after all, the service of preaching and the
sacraments remains central in church life. "What," it is
sometimes asked, "is so sacred about eleven o'clock on
Sunday morning?" In reply, one must say that there is
nothing sacred about eleven o'clock, and that what usually
happens then may indeed happen on some other day of
the week. Yet the service in which Jesus Christ is preached,
and his sacraments are administered, is what gives meaning to every other good thing that goes on in the church.
In fact, it is the preaching and sacraments that calls the
other activities into existence in the first place.

John Calvin wrote: "Wherever we find the word of God
purely preached and heard, and the sacraments administered according to the institution of Christ, there, it is
not to be doubted, is a church of God." (*Institutes of the*

*Christian Religion,* IV. 1. ix.) This definition of what constitutes a true church has become classical in our branch of Protestantism. We may take this as the starting point for understanding what the real church is and how it operates. Everything else is to be seen as following from these most basic elements of church life; and unless we grasp their importance, it may become increasingly difficult to believe that anything else about the church is important.

THE WORD PURELY PREACHED

The Reformation rose on the wings of preaching. Preaching was no Protestant invention, for from the first the disciples of Christ had gone into their communities and into far lands to preach. Without something to *say,* and without a message that other men could lay hold of and *believe,* there never would have been any church at all.

Throughout the Middle Ages preaching had its occasional glories, but on the whole it was buried under the ceremonial of the Mass and the "visual aids" (images, paintings, etc.) that medieval art and architecture provided to instruct an illiterate population. But when the Reformation got under way, the meaning of it was carried far and wide through Protestant pulpits. Luther, who asserted that all believers are priests, nevertheless was very emphatic in his claims for the authority of preaching. In one of his sermons he says: "This is what is meant by 'Thy king cometh.' You do not seek him, but he seeks you. You do not find him, he finds you. For the preachers come from him, not from you; their sermons come from him, not from you; your faith comes from him, not from you; everything that faith works in you comes from him, not from you; and where he does not come, you remain outside; and where there is no Gospel there is no God. . . ." [1]

Luther presumably knew that there was a difference between a good sermon and a bad one, and that of many a
sermon it could not reasonably be said that it came directly from God. No preacher, according to Reformation
doctrine, would be able to preach with the infallibility
that Roman Catholics ascribe to their church's utterances.
Moreover, by Protestant standards, it would be open to
congregations to have something to say about whether or
not they were hearing the gospel. What, then, is the significance of this bold statement by Luther? And what
is the meaning of the boldness, the authoritativeness, with
which Calvin and other Reformers constantly preached?
Why did some of the early Reformation churches, includ-
ing Calvin's, have preaching services several times a week?

The point is, first of all, that a sermon is not merely
another speech, designed to please the audience. It is the
means by which God has especially chosen to drive home
his message to men. What is spoken in a sermon is ideally
God's word, not simply human words arranged in an ear-
catching way or words that simply echo what the congregation already thinks. Even if this intention is not ideally
carried out by the preacher, yet by its very nature preaching is supposed to represent what God has to say to a
congregation. If it totally fails to do this, then it is false
or empty preaching, which is no preaching at all. The
direction is *from God to men*. The preacher is merely
God's instrument to proclaim the gospel of the forgiveness
of sins, and the obligations that this gospel imposes.

Normally the preacher functions by expounding Scripture—that is, by making the meaning of Scripture clear

---

[1] From Luther's *Church Postil*, Vol. I. Translated by Prof. John
Nicholas Lenker, D.D. Copyright, 1905, by Prof. J. N. Lenker, D. D.

and showing how it applies to the particular situation in which it is preached. The Reformation opened up the Bible to all the people. It did so, not only by translating it into common language so that everyone could read it for himself, but also by stressing the need for having its meaning and special force ever and again set forth through preaching. This point of view is reflected in The Shorter Catechism:

"Q. 89. How is the Word made effectual to salvation?

"A. The Spirit of God maketh the reading, but *especially the preaching,* of the Word an effectual means of convincing and converting sinners, and of building them up in holiness and comfort, through faith unto salvation."

In Calvin's classic definition, already quoted, we need to note further that he says, "Wherever we find the word of God purely preached *and heard . . .*" The hearing is not to be understood as a merely passive act on the part of the people, as though congregations were nothing more than sounding boards for their ministers' private opinions. When the word of reconciliation is proclaimed from the pulpit, the congregation is as much a part of the act as the preacher is. The sermon is not to be regarded as simply the minister's opportunity to express himself. What he is called and set apart to express is not *himself,* but the good news of the forgiveness of sins and the resurrection of the dead through Christ Jesus. To take hold of this, to rejoice in this, and to see the implications of this, is the privilege and duty of the congregation. The people are present in the first place because they have heard tidings of these things. To grasp, think about, and follow through on what is specifically said by the preacher is fully as active a part as the preaching of the sermon.

### THE SACRAMENTS RIGHTLY ADMINISTERED

Preaching, then, has been and continues to be at the center of church life. Regular public worship, without preaching, would be inconceivable in our Protestant tradition, for without the preaching it is not evident why people would be in church at all. They have been claimed for the church by the very word that is declared ever afresh from the pulpit.

With preaching, however, Calvin and the other Reformers joined the sacraments in the closest possible connection. Calvin, indeed, wished for the sacrament of the Lord's Supper to be observed every Sunday. If the reaction of the Genevan authorities against everything that seemed "Romanish" had not defeated Calvin's purpose, and made the celebration of this sacrament infrequent, our whole heritage of Reformed Church worship might have been very different from what we think of as normal. At any rate, the sacraments of Baptism and the Lord's Supper were exalted in Reformation thinking, these being the two that were instituted by our Lord. This is in contrast to the seven rites which Roman Catholics regard as sacraments (baptism, confirmation, the Eucharist, penance, holy orders, matrimony, and extreme unction).

What, then, is a sacrament? Calvin puts it very simply when he writes: "The sacrament therefore is an external sign through which the Lord presents and testifies to us his good will toward us in order to sustain us in the weakness of our faith. Or (to speak more briefly and more clearly) the sacrament is a testimony of the grace of God declared by an external sign."

This is very unlike popular views of Baptism as a "dedication of the child," and of the Lord's Supper as a mere "memorial feast" to recollect Jesus' death. In these popular views, it is man who takes the initiative and makes the approach to God. In Calvin's view, *God* takes the initiative and presents us with something that benefits us in our weak condition. The sacrament, in other words, is an act of God, administered duly by human hands. Here we may remind ourselves of what Luther said of preaching: "The preachers come from him, not from you; their sermons come from him, not from you; your faith comes from him, not from you . . ." As in preaching, so in the sacraments God reaches out toward us. If, therefore, sermon and sacrament are at the heart of worship, then worship cannot be interpreted as man's search for God. Further, we see why this worship is at the heart of all that the church is commissioned to do.

Even more clearly than preaching, however, the sacraments are acts of God. Preaching can easily be corrupted through the frailty of the human vessels that convey it. A preacher can utterly distort what is supposed to be the word of God. Sacraments, too, can be so distorted as to be mere caricatures of what God intends—as in the Roman Mass, so remote from the New Testament Lord's Supper, or as in "dedication" and "memorial" ceremonies in which there is no sense of God's doing anything. Yet, aside from such gross departures from the right celebration of the sacraments, we may say that God has in water and bread and wine provided means through which he may come to us directly. Granted due propriety in the conduct of the sacramental acts, we have here a way by which God has guaranteed his own access to men. Here are means of grace that man cannot ultimately corrupt: for the bread and wine are God's, through which (as Calvin taught) Christ is present to us spiritually; and the water on an infant's head is the simplest of ways by which God himself may signify that this child is of his family, and no man can pluck him out of the Father's hand.

To say that the sacraments belong to God, and that he

uses them to come to us directly, is at the opposite pole
from saying that they do their work automatically, or that
they are at the disposal of priests who have the power to
manipulate them. Here again we do well to consult The
Shorter Catechism (Q. 91) to help us tread the straight
and narrow way in our interpretation: "The sacraments
become effectual means of salvation, not from any virtue
in them, or in him that doth administer them, but only
by the blessing of Christ, and the working of his Spirit in
them that by faith receive them." To say that they are
God's, and therefore at *his* disposal, is to ascribe to him
alone the decision as to what will come of the administration of the sacraments and the power to make them fruit-
ful. The God who offers himself to us in the elements re-
serves his freedom at all times to give, to withhold, and to
take away.

## WHAT ELSE OF WORSHIP?

We have dealt at length with preaching and the sacraments as the cone of Christian worship. Once the basic
nature of these is understood, the place of other elements
in public worship becomes apparent. In sermon and sacrament God comes to us, offering us ever anew his word of
promise and forgiveness, and as it were thrusting his
gospel upon us in Baptism and the Lord's Supper. *Prayer
is our response to what God has been saying to us all along.*
As Christian congregations we pray for the pardon already
offered to us in the gospel. We pray in thankfulness for all
the mercies of God toward us. We pray that others also
may receive such gifts and graces as are made available to
us.

Hymns are, as a rule, a form of prayer—prayer put into
song. In hymns we praise God, petition him, ask for forgiveness, remember others; or commit ourselves anew to

him who has brought us once more under the shadow of his wing. The anthems sung by a choir likewise present some form of praise or prayer; and the organ is played, not to create "a worshipful mood," but to honor God with the riches of suitable musical art. The same, we should note, may be said of good church architecture: its intent is not primarily to play on the emotions of the worshipers, but simply to employ the arts and crafts to make an appropriate place for worship.

The offering, too, belongs as part of man's response to God's word. In preaching we are told of him who gave us all things, even himself; and in sacrament God again, as Calvin puts it, "presents and testifies to us his good will toward us." The Roman Mass seeks in some way to offer anew the sacrifice made once for all on Calvary. In our worship, all that we can offer is ourselves, of which some portion of our substance is a suitable token. Moreover, lest the symbolical side of the offering obscure the practical intention, it must be said that the offering of money is made with a conscious recognition that the church requires money in order to do its work in the world.

### THE PRIVATE WORSHIP OF THE CONGREGATION

Public worship has been the theme of this chapter. Yet it is to the point to speak here of private worship also, for public and private worship are inseparably joined. When a man goes into his own room to read the Bible, to meditate, to pray, he is doing this as a member of a Christian congregation. He is engaging in private worship, that is to say, because he has first of all been laid hold of by the word of grace that is spoken and given in public. He does not worship privately as the member of a secret or solitary cult. He is not sufficient to himself in his worship. He is compassed about with a great cloud of witnesses—witnesses who have persuaded him of the truth of the Christian faith and have made him one of them.

The Christian, like every other man, has his moments of extreme aloneness—the loneliness of hard decisions, above all, the ultimate loneliness of death. Yet he is not alone. He thinks, he acts, he decides, he even dies, as one of a mighty host. The reason for his private worship lies in what has been openly proclaimed and rejoiced in by the great congregation. When he prays alone, the church prays with him. When God speaks to him in secret, it is with the same voice that the man has heard before where the church gathers at the feet of Christ.

# CHAPTER 8

# Jesus Christ Is Lord: In the Church

The United Presbyterian Church acknowledges only one king and head. The Confession of Faith puts the matter very pungently: "The Lord Jesus is the only head of the church, and the claim of any man to be the vicar of Christ and the head of the church, is unscriptural, without warrant in fact, and is a usurpation dishonoring to the Lord Jesus Christ." (Ch. XXV, Sec. 6.)

This, of course, is aimed at the Roman Catholic Church, with its claim that the pope is "the vicar of Christ" on earth, but on the positive side this statement also highlights the principle that controls our whole church order; The United Presbyterian Church is organized democratically, so that Christ may rule and reign over us in his sovereign authority. This is an authority which can be delegated to no living person.

In view of what was said in the preceding chapter, as to the centrality of preaching of the Word and the sacraments, a question at once arises. It is this: If the Word and sacraments are central in our church life, does not this fact give to the ministry a kind of authority not unlike that of the Roman Catholic priesthood? The answer becomes an emphatic "No" when the nature of preaching is understood. A sermon, in the Protestant sense, is not an authoritative deliverance that is to be accepted as true simply because the preacher says so. On the contrary, it is an exposition of the Word of God, which the faith of the people must either accept as true and meaningful, or else reject as false and empty. When preaching is, as Calvin puts it, "pure," Christ uses the sermon as a means whereby he may express himself, though in the very imperfect words of the preacher. The truth of the sermon does not depend upon whether or not the congregation agrees with it. Christ often speaks through unpopular words. Yet there is nothing about the official position of the minister that makes his every word gospel truth. In the sacraments, Christ, as it were, takes over, and what is accomplished through the sacraments is by his will and blessing, not by virtue of the fact that a minister chose to go through a certain ritual. In both preaching and the sacraments, *God acts.*

## THE OFFICERS OF THE CONGREGATION

Although our church has no clerical class, with special prerogatives or supernatural authority, among the officers of the church the minister has a certain priority. This is expressed thus in the Form of Government of our church: "The pastoral office is the first in the church, both for dignity and usefulness." Among the various titles for this office which our Form of Government draws from Scripture, two are most common and most significant: pastor and minister. Both these terms imply the very opposite of special prerogatives. As pastor, a man called to this office is required, like the repentant Peter, to feed the flock with spiritual food. The term "minister" implies service.

Due weight, however, must be given to the fact that this office is considered "the first in the church." This is implemented, not by mere exhortations to honor the minister who discharges his duties faithfully, but by the actual form of church government. He is "first" in the administration of the local church. The minister presides over the session, which exists to oversee the life of the congregation. He is usually moderator of the board of deacons; and he may at his discretion attend meetings of the trustees, who are appointed to hold the titles to properties and to conduct other legal transactions on behalf of the congregation. But he is not "employed" by any of these groups, or even solely by the congregation. He is placed over a particular church by the presbytery (to be described later), acting co-operatively with the congregation. The presbytery is likewise involved in any change in pastoral relationships, and, when occasion demands it, in matters of friction between the congregation and its pastor.

These provisions in regard to the minister are made, not to exalt the man who is called to be servant of all, but to provide him with the necessary freedom for exercising his ministry as an ambassador of Christ. He is "first" for the sake of declaring the Word of God—responsible to God and to the church at large.

Yet the freedom of the people to live and work together as a congregation of Christ is just as fully provided for. The minister is not the only ordained officer of the congregation. In any United Presbyterian Church there are also *ruling elders,* ordained very much as pastors are. The ruling elders, meeting together as the session, form the governing body and hold responsibility for the whole life of the congregation. The session has the power to receive and to dismiss members, to supervise church worship and music, the Christian education program of the church, such groups as the Women's Association and the Men's Council, and the use of church properties. In connection with the ruling elders, our Form of Government significantly states the democratic principle underlying our whole church order: "Ruling elders are properly the representatives of the people, chosen by them for the purpose of exercising government and discipline, in conjunction with pastors or ministers."

Nor are the ruling elders the only ordained lay officers of the congregation. Most Presbyterian congregations also have deacons, who, like ruling elders and ministers, are ordained. Originally, the main function of the deacons was to take care of the poor and in other ways to minister to those in need. An amendment to our Form of Government, recently adopted, makes it possible for the deacons to have delegated to them responsibilities "relating to the oversight of members, to the finances and properties of the church, and to its evangelistic, missionary, and educational programs." Such delegation is given by the session, which retains primary responsibility for congregational life.

Boards of trustees function under the direction of the session and of the congregation as a legal corporation (in those states where it is proper for the church to be incorporated).

Although the authority of these officers of the congregation is very broad, it cannot be arbitrary. It must be carried out in accordance with the rules and regulations of The United Presbyterian Church. A person desiring to unite with The United Presbyterian Church must be received by the session. However, the session cannot for whimsical reasons, or through any prejudice, discriminate against prospective church members, for there are only two basic conditions for membership in The United Presbyterian Church, namely, acceptance of Jesus Christ as Savior and Lord, and a profession of willingness to follow his commandments. Here again, we see that the *headship* of Christ, and not the arbitrary authority of any group of persons, is what Presbyterian church order seeks to establish. Who, except Christ himself, can pass upon the faith of anyone who presents himself for church membership, whatever his background, race, color, or doctrinal views on nonessential matters?

THE JUDICATORIES OF THE CHURCH

No particular congregation by itself is the whole church. It is part of the structure of The United Presbyterian Church in its entirety. Presbyterian church order tries to express the unity of the church in its wholeness. In respect to church government, the particular congregation fits into the scheme of things depicted on the chart on page 92. Here we shall note briefly the main judicatories (or courts) of our church and their essential functions.

1. *The presbytery* is an organization provided for the churches in a certain district. Each congregation is represented in presbytery by its minister and by one of the ruling elders who is elected by the session. Although the presence of retired ministers or ministers not in pastoral work may mean that there are more ministers than laymen in any given presbytery, the intention is to provide such a balance as will prevent the church from being dominated by clergymen.

Broadly speaking, the functions of the presbytery are these: to ordain candidates to the ministry; to strengthen the work of the whole church within the bounds of the presbytery; to bind the local congregations in the program of the church as a whole; to approve calls to the ministry; to approve terms under which a minister is employed; to organize, merge, or dissolve churches; to assume control of the financial assets of a congregation that has been dissolved; to exercise discipline over the congregations and ministers under the jurisdiction of a particular presbytery.

The presbytery is responsible for seeing to it that the program of the whole church, as decided upon by the General Assembly, is carried out in the congregations within its bounds.

2. *Synods* are organizations of groups of presbyteries. As a rule, synod boundaries correspond with state boundaries. Each church in the area sends its pastor and one ruling elder to synod meetings. In the case of some of the larger synods, where it is not practicable to have every congregation represented, delegations of ministers and ruling elders are elected by the presbyteries. These delegates are called "commissioners."

The main functions of the synod are as follows: to review the records of presbyteries; to erect new presbyteries as needed; to subdivide or consolidate presbyteries; to receive appeals, complaints, and references that come from the presbyteries, deciding these except where the questions involve the doctrine or Constitution of the church, and to send the latter kind of reference on to the General Assembly; to supervise work involving more than one of the presbyteries within its bounds. Synods usually meet annually, for a period of about three or four days.

3. The *General Assembly* is the highest judicatory of the church. It meets once a year, and its commissioners are elected by the presbyteries. Each presbytery may send one minister and one ruling elder for each 7,000 ministerial and communicant members enrolled in that presbytery.

The General Assembly is the chief judicial, legislative, and executive body within The United Presbyterian Church. It hears appeals and receives references that have come up from lower judicatories; it reviews records; it decides controversies; it elects boards and agencies (later to be described); it proposes amendments to the Constitution of the church, and passes these back to the presbyteries to secure their vote upon such proposals; it erects new synods as they may be required. In a word, the General Assembly supervises the work of the whole church. It should be noted that here there is a perfect balance between ministers and laymen.

## BOARDS AND AGENCIES OF OUR CHURCH

Essential as this system of judicatories is, presbyteries, synods, and General Assembly could not by themselves carry out the continuing program of our church. The work of Jesus Christ cannot be carried on simply by passing motions or acting on resolutions. It is necessary, therefore, for General Assembly to create boards and agencies to enable the church, year in and year out, to carry out essential parts of the entire church's program. The election of board members, it should be noted, is thoroughly democratic, as is the life of our whole denomination; steps are taken to insure that ministers cannot dominate the conduct of these boards and agencies.

One agency, of great importance, is called the General Council. This is subject to the authority of the General Assembly and is charged with such duties as these: to supervise the spiritual and material interests of the boards of the church; ". . . to prepare and submit annually to the General Assembly (1) the budget for the permanent benevolence and missionary agencies of the church . . . ." It is also asked to co-ordinate the missionary and benevolence programs of the church as proposed by its boards, and to promote Christian stewardship throughout the church.

The agency known as the Council on Theological Education enables the seminaries, at which most Presbyterian ministers are trained, to co-ordinate their work.

When we come to the boards, we find that they are four in number, as indicated on the chart on page 92. It is essential to realize that these are not bureaucratic organizations, acting in a vacuum. Rather, they are arms of the church for carrying out the will and work of Jesus Christ in their several spheres of responsibility.

One board, administering a system of old-age pensions for ministers and other salaried workers in the church, has, for more than thirty years, been laboring to relieve the danger of destitution in old age that confronts those who enter professional church work.

The other three boards are all, in a sense, "mission" boards, acting in obedience to the command of Christ: "Make disciples of all nations, . . . teaching them to observe all that I have commanded you." Two of these work, respectively, in the sphere of national missions here at home and in the Christian mission abroad. The third, devoted to Christian education, likewise endeavors to give the resources and leadership necessary for the teaching task to which The United Presbyterian Church has from its beginning been dedicated. In India or Korea, as in America, the gospel must be preached and the ministry of healing must be offered. As part of the world church, working through an appropriate board, every Presbyterian in the United States can collaborate with his Christian brethren in such far places, and in return enjoy the fellowship and ministrations of the churches that have sprung up all over the world. Within our own land, we see congested cities where vast numbers of people have never darkened a church door, and great rural spaces with churches too weak to support themselves. Here again, through appropriate action by a board, problems of slum dwellers, isolated rural residents, migrants, refugees, and others can be confronted by each and every Presbyterian of our church. Again, who is to develop teaching materials and training programs for the church at large—demands exceeding what any particular congregation can fulfill with its own resources? Who is to put forth a churchly effort in the realm of higher education, so that teachers and students in university centers may feel the touch of Christ? Once more, it requires the effort of the church through its appropriate board to accomplish such aims.

The boards are not isolated from the life of the congregations. From the congregations of our church come the necessary financial contributions, the prayer, the moral support, and the human leadership that make it possible for Christ to reign as king over immense areas of human need. From the congregations of our church come also the members of the boards; and from the congregations are recruited the ministers and lay people who staff our boards. "Give, and it will be given to you," Jesus said. What goes forth from the congregation into these ever greater expanses, whether by way of monetary gifts or spiritual concern, returns to bless and strengthen each church member.

This is all one work. Where Christ's compassion, his concern, is allowed to dominate, his rule becomes apparent near and far. Like a stone cast into the water, the Word of God creates infinitely broadening circles of effect. "Jesus shall reign"—in what is done at the service of worship, through the various organizations of the congregation, through judicatories, through boards; all this joyful labor springs from *his* compassion and commandments, declared to us by the gospel that called our church into being.

THE LARGER CHURCH

If no congregation can live to itself, neither can any denomination live to itself. It would not be characteristic of The United Presbyterian Church to be satisfied with its own efforts and achievements. This church order of ours which tries to be broad enough for the whole scope of God's word and will also calls upon us to look beyond ourselves. But through what means can we be effective beyond the restricted sphere of our daily activities?

You are an individual who, through one means or another, has been brought within hearing distance of God's good word of grace in Jesus Christ. You are ready to make your profession of faith in Christ and to submit your ways to him; but by this very decision you place yourself within the company of many others in a congregation who have responded to the same call. Already, you have ceased to be alone in whatever you do as a disciple of the Lord Jesus Christ.

As a member of a congregation, you find next that your congregation is not alone either. If it is within The United Presbyterian Church U.S.A., it is one of between nine and ten thousand other congregations held together in a nationwide scheme of operation. You find that your congregation is joined with others, in the same area, in a presbytery; and, in a larger area, in a synod. You find that the whole denomination of which you are now a part is annually represented by a General Assembly. You find that the ongoing work of your church, through the length and breadth of the land, is supplied with help and leadership through boards and agencies, and that all this is *your* work, to which you contribute, and from which you receive.

But the story does not stop here. The United Presbyterian Church U.S.A. is a member of the National Council of the Churches of Christ in the United States of America—an organization through which most of the major denominations of this country co-operate. The things that they do together amount to more than publishing pieces of

literature and organizing conventions. Through their uni-
fied efforts, the member denominations try, as one body,
to make the voice of the church heard above all the other
raucous voices that cry out so loudly. Together, the
churches of this country endeavor to encourage the love
of peace and the hatred of war, to stimulate support for
the United Nations, to create happy homes, to do something for delinquent youth, and, above all, to seek to bring
men and women into the church of Jesus Christ. All of
this is too great for any one church that prefers to work
alone. It is, indeed, too great for all the churches together;
but Christ, the head of the whole church will not abandon
or forsake what is undertaken in his name.

But this country is only one of many; and throughout
the civilized world, the church has at least a foothold. To
make the most of that foothold is the duty of the World
Council of Churches, of which our United Presbyterian
Church is a member. In continuing, ongoing work, and
not merely in periodic assemblies, the World Council of
Churches wrestles with the question of how to minister
to the hungry, the suffering, and the uprooted across the
face of the earth. It is busy studying the great questions of
theology—age-old questions—that agitate the minds of
men, and sometimes keep churches apart. It looks for
ways to maintain fellowship with Christians in countries
politically separated from ours by our great modern wars
of ideologies.

What will come of these ambitious efforts to grapple
with the terrifying issues of human life, the Head of the
universal church alone knows. In the effort, however, you
have a part by virtue of the fact that you took your place
among the people of the congregation in your own city or
village. You have a part, because there is one Head and
one alone for all the church throughout the world, and

allegiance to the King of us all makes each one of us a part of something greater than himself. "But if any man draw back, my soul shall have no pleasure in him." (*Heb. 10: 38*, KJV.)

# CHAPTER 9

# Jesus Christ Is Lord:
# In the Common Life

We sometimes have a way of speaking of "the church" as though it consisted of anybody and everybody except ourselves. "This is the task of the church," we say; or, more vehemently, "Why doesn't the church do something about it?" If we are inside and not outside the church, such comments refer to our own responsibilities, not to an impersonal institution in which we have no part and from which we can stand aloof.

The loyalty of the church to its Lord means, in the last resort, the loyalty of the persons who are members of the body of Christ. For us there is no church "way out there," earning our applause or our criticism, as the occasion warrants. Christ will take care of the praise or the reproof; in either case, it is we who are judged.

Yet the individual might be justified in feeling somewhat detached from the church if he had no way of engaging in the Christian warfare save through the organizations that have been described. The issue must come closer home, in order to give meaning to the Christian life each and every day. A comparison may be found in citizenship. America is busy in matters of foreign policy: endeavoring, for example, to meet communism with a better way of life, and if possible to prevent total war. As a citizen of a democracy, each American can rightly feel that he has a share in forming national policy. Yet he is only one of many millions. Can he express good citizenship in no way except through his single vote, or, if he is more than usually articulate, in making his views known either to government officials or the public as a whole? Actually, every political word he speaks in private contributes to peace or war, to discord or international understanding. Then, beyond things that are directly political, he has decisions to make every day as to integrity in his business, good workmanship in his labor, the relationships within his home, which all profoundly affect the level of citizenship in this country.

In the church every member has opportunity to make some contribution—in proportion to his own resources—to the strategy of the church in meeting the problems of the world. It is an opportunity that excites the imagination; and it is offered, not merely to the few, but to all. The world-wide work of the church has not been pre-empted by the so-called "leaders." It is not only the right, but the duty, of the local congregation to make its weight felt in things of public concern. In this most accessible and intimate of organizations, Christians can and must stand together.

Yet the Lordship of Jesus Christ is not expressed solely in matters of grand strategy. Our battle front, as church members, is not defined simply by the policies of the congregation, of the General Assembly, of boards and agencies, of the National Council of Churches, of the World Council of Churches. Not one of these organizations could take account—except in the most general terms—of the countless battle fronts on which the individual Christian must daily fight in the service of the church's Lord.

## THE "TODAY" OF DECISION

Every Christian has innumerable spheres of action. It is up to *him* to make decisions continually—decisions that reflect obedience or disobedience to our Lord. Like every alien who visits a foreign country, he is a kind of ambassador who represents his Lord well or badly, and gives a good or bad impression of the church. He can never pass on to officers of the church the duty of carrying out Christ's commandments. He can never look for love to be adequately put into action by church officials or church assemblies. For commandments are to be obeyed by persons; and what is so personal as love? No master plan could ever be devised that would relieve the individual of his responsibility to think, speak, and act as though the whole Kingdom of Christ were at stake in his attitudes and deeds.

It is as the letter to the Hebrews, speaking to every believer, says:

> "Today, when you hear his voice,
>    do not harden your hearts as in the rebellion,
>    on the day of testing in the wilderness. . . .

"But exhort one another every day, as long as it is called 'today.'" (*Heb. 3:7-8, 13.*)

"As long as it is called 'today'" points to the urgency of the task that awaits every Christian. There is no putting off any duty until some revolution in the congregation, in the church at large, or in the world, makes the reign of Christ apparent to everyone. TODAY—in this sinful, suffering, and threatened world, just as it is and not in some far-off millenium—the Christian is called to harken to God's demanding voice. Today we are faced with the decisions that have to be made, the actions that have to be taken, perhaps with the suffering that has to be endured. So far from shouldering this imperative today in our stead, the church insists that we take it seriously for ourselves. Before nightfall we shall have honored or grieved our Lord. Before there is another "today," each one of us will have had ample opportunity, within our common life, to have advanced or retarded all that the church is endeavoring to do.

### HUMAN DECISIONS AND CHRIST'S DEMANDS

What are the areas in which the individual must act—perhaps all by himself—in this ominous today? They are too many to be counted; too many, perhaps, even to be effectively illustrated. Here is a man struggling against the prejudices and blind fears of a whole community, so that a family of another race or color may be permitted to settle there. Here is another man, conscious of dishonesty in the place where he is employed, and yet afraid to protest because food and clothes for his family depend on his continued employment. Here, again, is someone who is aware of intense political passions being stirred up in the place where he must live and work; and he is torn between the desire to speak the truth as he sees it and his craving for acceptance in his social circle. Here is a young person, afraid to be himself and break with the "crowd" because the pressure to conform weighs so heavily upon him.

Or, in less dramatic circumstances, here is someone who must decide what proportion of his money to give to the church—which means how far he and his family are willing to give up what they want badly for the sake of what matters supremely. Here is a father or a mother, trying to decide how far to permit a young person to go his own way and learn life by hard experience; or how far still to protect that youth through advice, prohibitions, or skillful maneuvering of his affairs. Here is a husband or a wife, looking for the way to resolve tensions within the home. Here is anyone at all, struggling to fulfill the complex requirements of integrity, courtesy, self-respect, concern for others.

Along the road of life, countless decisions, great and small, have to be made. The obligations of the Christian life cannot be set down in a few simple rules; nor can they be reduced to a handful of pious regulations that leave the rest of life untouched. For Christ as Lord of life extends his authority in all directions. He is not satisfied to confine himself to a right way of worship, or the proper conduct of church affairs. He intrudes into politics, into schools, into hospitals, into the professions, into business, into labor unions, into social institutions. He insists on having his way in the home, so that romance and family love wither or are frustrated if they do not enjoy his continual blessing. Nowhere can one go to escape the imperious demands—and the wondrous self-offering of Jesus Christ. Thus at every turn of life, from birth to death, decisions have to be made that the Christian must interpret as decisions *for or against Jesus Christ*. The formal profession of faith in him counts for little if it bears no fruit in thoughts and words and deeds that are shaped by the fear of God.

### THE CHURCH AND THE INDIVIDUAL

The decisions of which we have been speaking must be made by each man or woman personally. Yet in the making of them no one is absolutely alone, lonely though the circumstances may be. It was pointed out in the case of worship that when the individual prays in secret he nevertheless prays as a member of the Christian congregation, and the whole church prays with him. Similarly, in the daily decisions of the common life, the individual is supported by the church as a whole. He must, as a rule, think through for himself implications of Christian faith for his life. But he need not think them through as though no one had ever been concerned about them before. He is not on virgin soil.

How does the fact of the *church* and its witness help the individual in his private wrestlings? A number of ways may be suggested. In the first place, where particular issues are especially sharp, it may happen that the pulpit can and must speak to questions that are involved. Where, for example, some issue of race, or of civil liberties, is at stake, the preacher will not or ought not to be silent. Or, if the pulpit is not an appropriate place in which to speak of special problems, pastoral counseling or special discussion groups and forums may provide the aid that the Christian needs in his time of trial.

Then, in the literature issued or endorsed by a church, there may be expressed the Christian view on special issues. It is, in fact, a duty of those charged with preparing church literature of all kinds—anything from church school materials to special pamphlets—to deal pointedly with difficult questions and not evade them. The criticism that may be provoked by such pointedness is as nothing compared to the judgment of God—a judgment that falls with unusual severity on watchmen who fail to raise their voices when danger is near. Furthermore, it is the duty of judicatories of the church, and especially of the General Assembly, to make clear the position of the church on thorny matters. For example, the pronouncements of General Assembly in regard to social issues offer to the individual church and the individual believer a framework within which he can think through his own decisions. When General Assembly, for instance, alerts the church to the divisive forces that seek to thwart the United Nations, or when it opposes legalized gambling, or when it at one and the same time denounces communism and the hysteria called forth by anti-communism, such statements are not to be taken lightly. What General Assembly has to say does not have the binding authoritative force for Presbyterians that Vatican pronouncements have for Roman Catholics, but the highest court of our church may claim to express something that all members are bound to take seriously. Added to all this is the weight of Christian opinion, within and outside our church, on questions of ethics, society, and personal living.

What this means is that we are not simply individuals who happen to have come together in an organization called "the church." "We are members one of another." We are under the commandment to "bear one another's burdens, and so fulfil the law of Christ." We are not left to think everything through for ourselves, wholly with our own resources, lacking any administration from our brethren in Christ. Our most private, intimate, and personal decisions are all bound up with the life and thought of the church as a whole. What we decide, we decide as members of the church.

Yet when all of this is said, it must be acknowledged that in many and varied circumstances the decisions of life have to be made on our own responsibility, under the guidance of the congregation and the church as a whole, with the support of our fellow Christians, but in a personal way that does not provide anyone to stand at our elbows and tell us what we ought to do. Indeed, it must further be admitted that at times we must, in all conscience, resist both the counsel and the example of the church at large. There is an expression which, however colloquial it may be, describes the situation of many an individual: "going

out on a limb." It is just this willingness to stand alone
if need be, to take risks if necessary, to make up our own
minds on occasion, regardless of even church opinion, that
has from the beginning been characteristic of the Presbyterian Church. This is not mere "individualism." On the
contrary, this quality is what has enabled The United
Presbyterian Church to move ahead dynamically—never
standing still, with the consequent danger of freezing in
its tracks. Someone must take the chance and set the pace;
and if the decision be right, it will be the pioneer step that
guides the church where it ought to go. Just as, in many
situations, the words and deeds of others will minister to
us, so in some situations our own willingness to take up the
cross and follow Christ will, in the long run, minister to
the rest of the church. And even if what is said or done
should never be heeded, the faithfulness of the individual
will still glorify the church to which he belongs.

WHOSE DECISION?

These individual decisions in so many spheres are not,
we have said, mere individualism, for they are part of the
life and thought and strength of the entire church. There
is an even deeper reason for regarding our personal decisions as more than individualistic. If they are truly the
decisions of discipleship, then they are Christ's decisions,
and not ours. "Today, *when you hear his voice . . .*" It is
his voice that determines for us what must and must not
be done today.

This is not to say that Christ has necessarily endorsed,
much less inspired, our particular convictions. On the
contrary, the church member must be prepared to have
his own convictions (which are sometimes nothing more
than prejudices) continually disturbed. Into our lives,
with our self-assurance as to what is right and wrong, there

comes a voice from another realm than ours. It frequently tells us that we are mistaken and that we must decide another way. Frequently it reminds us that the decision we have reasoned out to our own satisfaction is not *his will* at all, but simply a rationalization of what we would like to think and do.

This strange voice may be heard through preaching, through teaching, through conversation, through printed studies, through our own meditation on the Scriptures. On the basis of all these things, it may, perhaps, be heard quite unexpectedly and inexplicably when we are faced with a decision that we have to make. When we are aware that there is a voice, calling our own standards into question, and coming to us in ways that we cannot analyze, we know what it is to be met by a Lord who is greater than we are and exalted above the church. This voice cuts across our desires, our hopes, our settled patterns of thought, our upbringing, with a message all its own. No one can say, in advance of any decision of daily life, where this voice may summon us, or what it may call us to do or to abhor.

We are not left to ourselves in any situation of loneliness. Faced by choices, we find that there is One who has anticipated our dilemmas and our needs. It is the Lord, who claims all of life as his domain. He will decide which way we ought to go. The decision will not be ours, but the Master's. Hearing him speak in the "still small voice," the disciple has no choice but to follow where he leads. The consequences must be left to take care of themselves. Our times are in his hand.

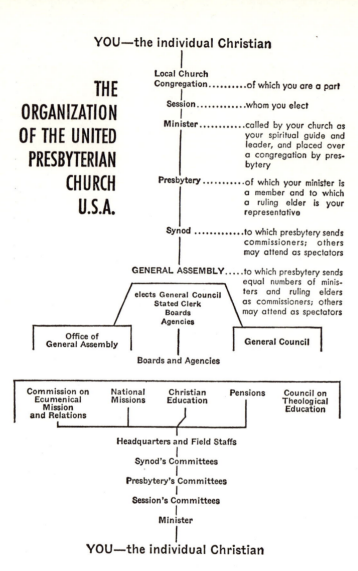

**YOU—the individual Christian**

THE ORGANIZATION OF THE UNITED PRESBYTERIAN CHURCH U.S.A.

Local Church
Congregation..........of which you are a part

Session............whom you elect

Minister............called by your church as your spiritual guide and leader, and placed over a congregation by presbytery

Presbytery...........of which your minister is a member and to which a ruling elder is your representative

Synod .............to which presbytery sends commissioners; others may attend as spectators

GENERAL ASSEMBLY.....to which presbytery sends equal numbers of ministers and ruling elders as commissioners; others may attend as spectators

elects General Council
Stated Clerk
Boards
Agencies

Office of General Assembly

General Council

Boards and Agencies

| Commission on Ecumenical Mission and Relations | National Missions | Christian Education | Pensions | Council on Theological Education |
|---|---|---|---|---|

Headquarters and Field Staffs

Synod's Committees

Presbytery's Committees

Session's Committees

Minister

**YOU—the individual Christian**